DISASTERS

ECOLOGICAL DISASTERS

ANN WEIL

SADDLEBACK
EDUCATIONAL PUBLISHING

DISASTERS

Air Disasters

Deadly Storms

Earthquakes

Ecological Disasters

Fire Disasters

Mountain Disasters

Sea Disasters

Space Disasters

Terrorism

Volcanoes

SADDLEBACK
EDUCATIONAL PUBLISHING
www.sdlback.com

ISBN-13: 978-1-61651-930-8
ISBN-10: 1-61651-930-4
eBook: 978-1-61247-626-1

Printed in the U.S.A.

21 20 19 18 17   4 5 6 7 8

Photo Credits: page 26, Bettmann/Corbis; page 17, Nik Wheeler/Corbis; page 37, Roger Ressmyer/Corbis; pages 39, 55, AFP/Corbis; page 47, Paul A. Souders/Corbis; page 48, Roy Corral/Corbis; pages 66–67, The Asahi Shimbun / The Asahi Shimbun / Getty Images; page 79, © Adelie-penguin | Dreamstime.com; page 88, © Bizoon | Dreamstime.com

CONTENTS

Chapter 1 | Introduction. 4

Chapter 2 | London, 1952 10

Chapter 3 | Love Canal, 1970s 20

Chapter 4 | Hanford, 1943. 30

Chapter 5 | *Valdez,* 1989. 40

Chapter 6 | Chernobyl, 1986 50

Chapter 7 | Bhopal, 1984 56

Chapter 8 | Fukushima Daiichi, 2011 62

Chapter 9 | Global Warming. 72

Chapter 10 | The Aral Sea 82

Glossary. 90

Index 92

DATAFILE

Timeline

June 22, 1969

Cuyahoga River in Cleveland, Ohio, catches fire due to its chemical pollution.

April 22, 1970

The first Earth Day is celebrated. Earth Day is a yearly event that reminds us to take care of the environment.

Where is Cleveland?

HERE

Key Terms

acid rain—rain that is harmful because it is mixed with polluted air

extinct—no longer alive

ozone layer—a part of the atmosphere that takes out some of the sun's harmful rays

pollution—something that harms the air, water, or soil

CHAPTER 1 | Introduction

Our planet is home to billions and billions of plants and animals. Living things need air and water to survive. They also need a place to live. This is their—and our—environment.

Pollution Threatens

Some disasters threaten our environment. Many are the result of pollution. Modern life produces a lot of wastes. We throw away garbage bags full of trash. A lot of this ends up in large dumps.

Water pollution kills fish and other animals. It can also make water unsafe to drink.

Fumes from cars pollute the air. Air pollution causes health problems for many people. It can also reduce the ozone layer high in Earth's atmosphere.

The ozone layer filters out some of the sun's harmful rays. Without this protection, more people may die of deadly skin cancers.

Air pollution also causes acid rain. Polluted air mixes with rain as it falls to the ground. Acid rain is a serious problem all over the world. It kills plants and animals.

Many species are becoming extinct because of acid rain. Acid rain also pollutes lakes. The fish in those lakes die. Acid rain can even wear away some old buildings.

We use wood to build homes and furniture. People also use wood to heat their homes. A lot of the world's paper supplies come from wood. That's a lot of trees! But forests are disappearing. Many species of rainforest plants and animals are becoming extinct.

These problems could turn into environmental disasters. Some environmental disasters build up over long periods of time. Others can happen in an instant.

Industrial Accidents

Industries use chemicals to make things we use everyday. Many of these chemicals are poisonous. Most industries are responsible and safe. But accidents do occur. Most industrial accidents are minor. Some are very serious. A few are environmental disasters.

What Can We Do? Recycle!

Recycling bottles, cans, and paper is one way to reduce pollution. And it's something we can all do to help our environment. Recycling saves fuel. Using less fuel means less air pollution, too.

CHAPTER 2 | London, 1952

DATAFILE

Timeline

December 4, 1952

A thick, yellow smog covers London, England.

July 5, 1956

In response to the smog, the United Kingdom passes the Clean Air Act.

Where is London?

Key Terms

asthma—a condition that sometimes makes it hard to breathe

industry—a business that uses machines and often produces a lot of pollution

smog—a mixture of smoke, chemicals, and fog

CHAPTER 2 | London, 1952

London is the capital city of England. It is also a very old city. People lived in London hundreds of years ago.

At first, people heated their homes with wood. Later, they switched to coal. They burned the coal in stoves. This made a lot of smoke.

In the 1800s, industries added to the air pollution. By the early 1900s, the air was very dirty. The people of London were used to the problem. They lived with smoky air for many years.

They didn't realize it was a killer waiting to strike.

What is Smog?

Smog is a mixture of smoke and fog. London is famous for its fog. The city is close to the sea. The air is moist. Fog is made up of tiny particles of water. It's like a cloud close to the ground.

London had fog long before the air became polluted. The fog had never been a problem before.

But smoke and fog can be a deadly combination. The air turns yellow-brown. It is hard to breathe. The smog can get so thick, it's even hard to see.

Smog can cause health problems. It can damage the lungs. It can cause some types of cancer. It can also make some illnesses much worse.

People with asthma are badly affected by smog. People with heart disease are more likely to suffer a heart attack.

Fifty years ago, people were not so aware of the dangers of smog. It took a disaster to force them to clean up their act.

The Great Smog

On December 4, 1952, a yellow cloud of smog covered London. It got worse and worse. Cars crawled through the streets. Drivers could see only a few feet ahead. Movies were canceled. People could not see the screen.

Everyone noticed the smog was bad. But there were no warnings on the radio or television. At first, people did not realize this was an emergency.

Farm animals became sick and died. More people than usual were going to the hospitals. The smog was to blame.

The Great Smog lingered for five days. Finally it blew away. But not before it killed 4,000 people. Most died of lung and heart illnesses. Thousands more people died later from the effects of the smog.

The Great Smog forced London to address its air pollution problem. The government passed its first Clean Air Act in 1956.

People used cleaner fuels. Less smoke went into the air. London still has smog. But these changes have kept the Great Smog a thing of the past.

Los Angeles, 1970s

Los Angeles has a smog problem. It is one of the smoggiest cities in the United States.

Exhaust from millions of cars and trucks becomes trapped over the city by the Santa Monica and San Gabriel mountains. The smog was at its worst in the 1970s. Then laws were passed to reduce car fumes. This helped lower smog levels.

The Los Angeles smog

Meuse Valley, Belgium, 1930

There were many glass factories and other industries in the Meuse Valley. They produced a lot of smoke. In December, there was unusual weather. The pollution was trapped close to the ground.

The smoke mixed with a thick misty fog. Within a few days, the smog made more than 600 people very sick.

People with heart problems and bad lungs were especially affected. But some young people also became seriously ill. About 60 people died.

Donora, Pennsylvania, 1948

America's first pollution tragedy occurred in the small town of Donora. There were many industries in Donora. These included a sulfuric acid plant, a steel mill, and a zinc production plant.

Pollution became trapped in the narrow valley. It mixed with fog. The smog affected almost half the population of Donora. About 6,000 people became ill. Some had sore throats. Others had headaches. Their eyes burned. There were 20 deaths in three days.

DATAFILE

Timeline

1896

William Love begins digging a canal near Niagara Falls, New York.

1942

A chemical company starts dumping toxic wastes into the canal.

Where is Niagara Falls?

Key Terms

contaminated—polluted or infected

pesticides—poisons used to kill animals, insects, or plants

toxic—very harmful

CHAPTER 3 | Love Canal, 1970s

In 1896, a man named William Love started digging a canal near Niagara Falls, New York. The canal was never completed. Instead, it became a huge dump. This place became known as Love Canal.

A Chemical Dumpsite

In the 1940s and early 1950s, a chemical company dumped about 21,000 tons of acids, pesticides, and other toxic wastes into the canal. The dump was closed in 1953.

The chemical company covered the area with clay. This was supposed to seal the chemicals inside. It looked like empty land. But the chemical waste was just below the surface.

The chemicals were inside large metal drums. Some of the drums were old and rusted. Many damaged drums split open when they were dropped into the dump.

Over the years, the drums broke down. More and more drums leaked. The chemicals seeped into the ground. These chemicals were known to cause cancer. They also caused birth defects. Some of the acids were strong enough to burn through skin.

People Move In

The city of Niagara Falls grew. More and more people moved there. The city needed to build a new school. They decided to build it over the chemical dump.

They began building in 1957. This broke the clay seal. Some of the chemicals ended up on the surface. School children playing in the dirt got burned. The chemicals irritated their skin.

New Homes are Built

By the 1970s, hundreds of families were living there. Most of them had no idea they were living on top of an environmental disaster.

Soon, many people who lived in the neighborhood of Love Canal had health problems. There were mysterious illnesses.

People seemed sick for no reason. The rate of miscarriages and birth defects was much higher than average. People developed liver and kidney disease.

In 1977, the air around Love Canal smelled funny. It was the chemicals.

The chemicals were turning up everywhere. They were in backyards. They flowed through creeks. They were even in people's basements. These toxic wastes had traveled from the dump into people's homes.

Grass wouldn't grow on some lawns. People got sick after eating vegetables from their own gardens.

Enough is Enough!

It isn't easy to prove that a dump is causing health problems. But one Love Canal resident was determined to do just that.

Lois Gibbs studied the problem. She organized the community. At first, the government refused to help. Eventually, they were forced to accept the facts. The dump was poisoning the people of Love Canal.

People were told to leave their homes. It cost over $30 million to evacuate the area. The residents were given money to move.

The message on the sign refers to the toxic chemicals in the ground below the porch of this home in Love Canal.

The Government Steps In

The government bought their houses. Many homes were torn down. Love Canal was declared a disaster area.

It took 20 years and $250 million to clean up Love Canal. The toxic waste is still buried there. There is a fence around the dump site.

The Love Canal disaster received a lot of attention. People all over America learned of the dangers of toxic wastes. They also discovered there were many more "Love Canals" all over the country.

Billions of dollars were spent cleaning up other contaminated areas. Some states passed laws to control how industries disposed of their wastes.

Now Love Canal has been tested. It has been declared a safe place to live. Love Canal is now called Black Creek Village.

Times Beach, Missouri, 1982

In 1982, the people of Times Beach made an awful discovery. A man named Russell Bliss had been paid to get rid of a load of dioxin.

Dioxin is a very poisonous chemical.

Bliss mixed the dioxin with waste oil. Then he sprayed it on dirt roads in Times Beach. He said it would control the dust. But it ended up destroying the town.

Dioxin does not break down in water or soil. It ended up in the Meramec River. Then the river flooded. The floodwater spread dioxin over the town. Times Beach became unlivable. Everyone had to leave. Times Beach was once home to about 2,000 people. Now it is a ghost town.

DATAFILE

Timeline

March 1943

The first nuclear power plant is built in Hanford, Washington. The plant makes plutonium for atomic bombs.

August 6, 1945

The United States drops the first atomic bomb on Hiroshima, Japan.

Where is Hanford?

HERE

Key Terms

atomic bomb—a weapon that causes a powerful, hot explosion

filter—a device that makes the air or water clean

radioactive—giving off energy as a result of the break-down of atoms

CHAPTER 4 | Hanford, 1943

In 1943, the first nuclear plant was built in Hanford, Washington. This plant made radioactive plutonium. This was an essential ingredient for building the atomic bomb.

Plutonium from Hanford was in the atomic bomb that ended World War II.

Over the years, Hanford produced enough plutonium for many nuclear weapons. It also produced tons and tons of deadly nuclear waste. By the 1980s, Hanford was an environmental disaster.

Nuclear weapons were first used in World War II. Scientists had known the theory behind an atomic bomb before then. But no one had made one. With the world at war, the pressure was on to build a better bomb.

In 1942, American scientists began working on a top-secret project. It was called the Manhattan Project. They wanted to build the first nuclear weapon.

The stakes were very high. Other countries were also rushing to build an atomic bomb. It was a race to see who would make one first. And whoever won this race would win the war.

The A-Bomb

The Americans won the race—and the war. The atomic bomb (or A-bomb) was the first nuclear weapon. It's called a nuclear weapon, because its power comes from the nucleus of an atom.

There is a lot of energy locked inside the nucleus of each tiny atom. The A-bomb releases this energy as tremendous heat and a huge shock wave. Buildings and people are burned to ashes. Deadly radiation contaminates the earth and water.

The A-Bomb exploded atoms of plutonium. Each bomb needed only about 13 pounds of plutonium. That's a piece of plutonium about the size of a baseball. It could produce an explosion capable of destroying an entire city.

Hanford: The Early Years

The Hanford nuclear plant was built in 1943. It produced most of the plutonium used in the first atomic bombs. It was the first plant of its kind. There were no safety standards for nuclear plants then. The scientists were focused on winning the war.

Radioactive materials were released into the air around Hanford. The first few years were the worst. But people did not know what was happening.

The government had said the plant was safe. But radiation is invisible. The amounts were never high enough to kill people immediately.

It wasn't until 1986 that the public learned the truth. The government finally released the information.

Between 1944 and 1947, large amounts of radioactive materials escaped into the air. Much of this was in the form of radioactive iodine. It went up the smokestacks of the reactor.

This problem was eventually solved. Special filters were put inside the smokestacks. The filters trapped the radioactive iodine. It no longer escaped into the air. The public was no longer exposed to high levels of radiation.

But another problem was not so easy to solve. The plant operated for about 50 years. It produced a lot of nuclear waste. There were 2,000 waste sites. A million pounds of radioactive uranium and plutonium were buried there.

About 60 million gallons of deadly radioactive wastes were buried in underground tanks. Some of these tanks leaked. Contaminated liquids ended up in the soil.

It will take many years to clean up Hanford. The government is still working out how to tackle this huge environmental mess. Some estimate it will take 40 years. When it is completed, the final chapter on this historic nuclear plant will have ended.

Hanford's reactor was completed in 1944 and soon began making plutonium that was used in the first atomic bombs.

Plutonium in Outer Space

There is radioactive plutonium on the moon. Astronauts left it there. It provides power for instruments on the moon's surface. Two pounds of plutonium generates enough heat to run the system for 80 years.

Nuclear technology also powers space exploration. Unmanned spacecraft (called probes) bound for Mars and Jupiter are powered by plutonium.

This shows the Mars Polar Lander (MPL) spacecraft on the Martian surface, in the South Polar Region.

CHAPTER 5 | *Valdez,* 1989

DATAFILE

Timeline

March 24, 1989

Exxon Valdez tanker spills 11 million gallons of crude oil in Prince William Sound, Alaska.

January 25, 1991

There is an oil spill of 1.5 million tons in Sea Island, Kuwait.

Where is Prince William Sound?

HERE

Key Terms

pipeline—a long line of tubes connected together

reef—rock or coral that is near the water's surface

tanker—a huge ship used to carry oil

CHAPTER 5 | *Valdez,* 1989

Most Americans use some kind of fuel oil every day. It powers our cars. It heats our homes. Oil is transported on huge ships called tankers. Tankers travel the globe. A single tanker can carry millions of gallons of oil. An accident can result in a disastrous oil spill.

That's what happened in Alaska in 1989. A tanker named the *Exxon Valdez* had just filled up with oil. It was on its way out of the port. The tanker was heading for California. But it didn't get very far.

Disaster Strikes

The accident happened just after midnight on March 24, 1989. The captain was asleep. The person steering the tanker was not experienced. There was floating ice in the bay. The crew changed course to avoid hitting it. But then they didn't correct their course.

The *Exxon Valdez* struck a reef. The rocks punched a hole in the ship. 11 million gallons of oil flowed out into Prince William Sound.

Wildlife Hit Hard

Waves and tides spread the oil. Some of the oil reached the shore. It ended up covering about 1,300 miles of the Alaskan coast.

The thick, black oil formed a sticky film over the beaches. Birds were the hardest hit. The total number of bird deaths will never be known. One estimate is as many as 250,000. Entire bird colonies were wiped out.

Thousands of rare sea otters were killed. Seals and killer whales also died from the oil.

Some animal populations bounced back, years later. There are as many bald eagles now as there were before the spill. But others never recovered.

Pink salmon was one of Alaska's best-selling fish. But salmon fishing was stopped after the spill. No one would buy salmon from polluted water.

For years, salmon eggs did not hatch properly. The oil spill was to blame. But this problem did not last forever. Over the years, the number of salmon increased. Salmon fishing started again.

Cleanup

Millions watched this drama on television. Pictures of birds covered in black crude oil were broadcast around the world. Many people volunteered.

But the cleanup was delayed. There were arguments over who would pay for it. The cleanup took three years. It cost more than $2 billion.

The ocean helped clean itself, too. Waves flushed out the oil. Sunlight and oxygen broke it down. But no cleanup is perfect. Prince William Sound is forever changed.

The *Exxon Valdez* was given a new name. It is now called the *SeaRiver Mediterranean*. It is still carrying oil around the world—but not to or from Alaska. The tanker is not allowed to enter Alaskan waters ever again.

Alaska Pipeline

The Alaska Pipeline (Trans-Alaska pipeline) goes from Prudhoe Bay to Valdez. Prudhoe Bay is the largest oil field in North America. Tankers can't go to Prudhoe Bay. It's too far north. There's too much ice in the water.

That's where the Alaska pipeline comes in. The oil is moved south along the Alaska pipeline. It ends up at Valdez. There, the oil is pumped onto tankers.

The pipeline is almost 800 miles long. Less than half of it is buried underground. The pipe itself has a diameter of 48 inches.

The Trans-Alaska pipeline is one of the largest pipeline systems in the world. There are 78,000 supports, spaced at 60-foot intervals, anchoring the above-ground sections.

A volunteer tends to a sea otter injured in the *Exxon Valdez* oil spill at the sea otter rescue center in Valdez, Alaska. The tanker ran aground on Bligh Reef in Alaska's Prince William Sound on March 24, 1989, spilling 11 million gallons of crude oil.

DATAFILE

Timeline

March 28, 1979

Radioactive gas escapes at Three Mile Island
nuclear power plant in Pennsylvania.

April 26, 1986

A nuclear reactor catches fire and burns for two
weeks in Chernobyl, a city in the Soviet Union.

Where is Chernobyl?

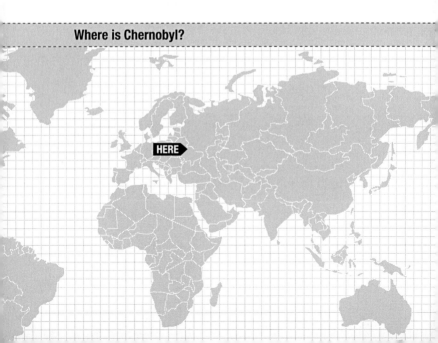

Key Terms

fallout—the radioactive particles that fall after a nuclear explosion

generate—to make

nuclear reactor—a device that produces nuclear energy

radiation—a form of energy that can cause cancer and other health problems

CHAPTER 6 | Chernobyl, 1986

There are nuclear power plants in many countries. They use nuclear energy to generate electricity. This electricity powers homes and businesses. People all over the world rely on nuclear power.

Most nuclear power plants operate safely. But an accident at a nuclear power plant can mean disaster.

Fire!

In April 1986, there was an explosion at a nuclear power plant in the Soviet Union. The nuclear reactor caught fire. The reactor burned for two weeks.

Firefighters risked their lives to put out the blaze. Tons of radioactive materials were blown into the air. The Russian government reported that

31 people died. Thousands more were exposed to high levels of radiation.

High doses of radiation may not kill someone immediately. But it can cause cancer and other health problems years later. More than 100,000 people who lived near the nuclear power plant were told to leave their homes. But the threat was not limited to Chernobyl.

Russian cities miles away were also affected. Radioactive dust fell on towns and cities miles away from the accident. Some cities hosed down the streets with water. They tried to rinse the dust away.

The nuclear fallout went beyond Russia. Radioactive ash and dust had formed a deadly cloud. Wind and rain pushed the cloud over Europe. It spread over 1,000 miles.

Sweden was the first European country affected. Farms there were ruined. The vegetables and soil were no longer usable. Even years after the accident, the ground was contaminated. Sheep in Scotland were also contaminated. So were reindeer in Finland.

What Caused the Explosion?

Workers at the Chernobyl nuclear power plant caused the accident. They turned off part of the machinery. The reactor heated up. Rods inside the reactor melted.

Uranium leaked into the water used for cooling the reactor. The water got boiling hot. Steam built up inside the reactor. The pressure of the steam blew up the top of the reactor.

It went through the roof of the power plant. There was a second explosion when cool air from outside came in contact with the red-hot core of the reactor.

Cleanup

Trees around the nuclear power plant were cut down. They were not burned. That might have made radioactive smoke. Everything was buried under concrete.

An engineer at the Chernobyl power plant turns off the last reactor, closing the plant that caused the world's worst nuclear accident.

DATAFILE

Timeline

December 3, 1984

Deadly gas leaks out of a pesticide factory in
Bhopal, India.

December 3, 1999

Environmental and human rights groups observe
the first "No Pesticides Day."

Where is Bhopal?

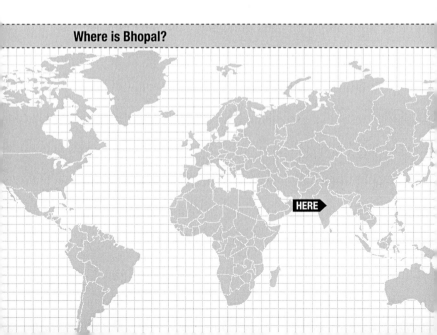

Did You Know?

Air currents carry pesticides long distances. In the cold Arctic region, the gas turns to solid. It ends up in the ice and snow. High levels of poisonous chemicals have been found in polar bears, seals, and people, too.

Key Terms

clinic—a place where doctors examine and treat patients

Union Carbide—a large company that owned the Bhopal pesticide factory

CHAPTER 7 | Bhopal, 1984

Some farmers use pesticides to kill insects that eat their crops. Chemical pesticides contain strong poisons. They are made in factories. An accident at a pesticide factory can be a disaster.

Poisonous Gas Escapes

In 1984, poisonous gas escaped from a pesticide factory in India. It was one of the worst industrial accidents ever.

A deadly cloud of gas swept over the city of Bhopal. Thousands of people were killed. Some died immediately after breathing the gas.

More than 8,000 died within 48 hours. Thousands more died later from the effects of the poison. The gas blinded some people instantly. Others had serious eye injuries.

The poison caused many health problems in the survivors. It damaged their lungs and other organs. This disaster seriously affected more than 80,000 people. And these awful effects are still with many of them today.

Fifteen Years Later

Even 15 years after the accident, survivors were still struggling. A clinic in Bhopal reported that 10 to 15 Bhopal survivors died each month. They also reported that 40 to 80 gas victims came to them every day for medical help.

The Bhopal pesticide factory was owned by Union Carbide. Union Carbide is a very large company. Some people blamed Union Carbide for the accident.

But the company claimed the accident was not their fault. They said an angry worker caused the accident on purpose.

Still, Union Carbide paid $470 million to the Indian government in 1989. Each victim was to receive about $500.

Some Indians feel this was not enough. Most of the victims were very poor. After the accident, they were too sick to work. They didn't have money to pay for medical help.

Doctors Still Seek Answers

Some doctors in Bhopal are still trying to find out more about the poison gas. They want to know which chemicals it contained. This may help them treat their patients better. They accused Union Carbide of keeping this information secret.

The fifteenth anniversary of the accident was on December 3, 1999. Human rights and environmental organizations made it a special day for action. They're working to make sure there are no more Bhopal disasters.

DATAFILE

Timeline

March 11, 2011

Japan is hit with a 9.0 magnitutde earthquake and massive tsunami within the span of one hour.

March 11, 2011

Reactors at Japan's Fukushima Daiichi nuclear power plant overheat and release radiation as a result of the earthquake and tsunami.

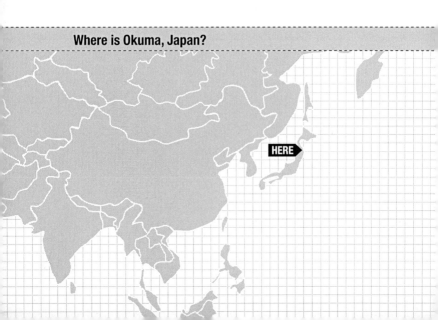

Where is Okuma, Japan?

HERE ▶

Key Terms

migratory—periodically migrating, meaning to pass from one climate or region to another

radiation—a form of energy that can cause cancer and other health problems

reactor—a device that produces nuclear energy

subatomic—particles contained in an atom, as electrons, protons, or neutrons

tsunami—an unusually large sea wave produced by an earthquake (In Japanese, *tsu* means harbor, and *nami* means wave.)

CHAPTER 8 | Fukushima Daiichi, 2011

There are more than 430 nuclear power plants in the world. Here in the United States, there are more than 100. Nearly 4 million Americans live within ten miles of a nuclear power plant. In the United States, 20 percent of our electricity comes from nuclear power.

Nuclear power plants emit low levels of radiation. Radiation is made up of subatomic particles. If people come into direct contact with these particles, our cells can be damaged. Cancer is one disease that can develop when radiation invades the human body.

The country of Japan ranks third in the world in number of nuclear power plants with 50. In 2011, one of them, the Fukushima Daiichi plant, was disabled by a powerful earthquake and tsunami.

An Earthquake. A Tsunami.
Then ... A Meltdown

On March 11, 2011, the Honshu Island of Japan was the scene of a devastating earthquake. At 2:46 p.m. local time, tremors hit 80 miles off the central coast of Sendai City in the Miyagi Prefecture. A huge 9.0 earthquake had occurred near the most populous island in Japan. Giant waves called tsunami resulted when the earth under the ocean shifted. The tsunami headed toward the coast.

The tsunami tore apart everything in its path. Cars and fishing boats were tossed like toys. Large ships were overturned by the tsunami's crushing power. Even houses were swept away.

Workers wear white hazmat suits and respirator masks in efforts to protect them against radiation.

The Fukushima Daiichi nuclear power plant was located just 180 miles north of Tokyo in the Fukushima Prefecture, near the town of Okuma (about 65 miles south of Sendai City). This plant was damaged by the combination of the earthquake and the tsunami. Inside, electric power shut down.

Water used to cool nuclear fuel rods heated up. A series of fires and explosions ripped through the plant. Radiation levels started to rise. Japanese authorities declared an emergency and ordered people to evacuate.

Scientists discovered that the fuel rods were damaged. Meltdowns in several reactors at Fukushima Daiichi released radiation into the surrounding air and water.

After the tsunami passed, many survivors were left trapped on the roofs of buildings. Some tried to escape by car. But roads and bridges were washed out. Dozens of rescue vehicles stalled on roads with nowhere to go. Patients trapped in hospitals had to be lifted out of the area by helicopter.

Overall, more than 20,000 people died or are still missing from the 2011 Japan earthquake and tsunami. Hundreds of thousands of residents were evacuated. Many of these men, women, and children will never see their homes again. Some do not want to go back. Their homes are gone, and the ground is so contaminated they cannot rebuild. People fear that their local food and milk will be tainted.

Nearly 90,000 people located near the Fukushima plant lost their homes. Millions of tons of debris have been cleaned up. But removal of contaminated material will take years. The accident has caused many in Japan to consider more clean energy technologies like wind, solar, and geothermal. In Spring of 2012, the last operating nuclear power plant in Japan was shut down. The government is still considering whether to bring them back on line ever again.

It Could Have Been Worse

Japanese residents regularly participate in emergency warning drills. Japan also has strict building codes. Unfortunately, many older homes in Japan were not up to code and were destroyed. Because of this tragedy, the people of Japan are demanding that future buildings and roads be constructed to withstand the next earthquake. This is a critically important issue. Scientists estimate an up to 70 percent chance that a magnitude 7.0 earthquake or higher will hit Tokyo in the next four years.

Japanese officials admitted they were not prepared for such a devastating tsunami. Sea walls built to keep out the waves were only ten feet high in Sendai City, near where the quake was centered. Despite having a major fault line just offshore, the sea wall at Fukushima was less than 20 feet high. The actual height of the tsunami wave at Fukushima was over 45 feet.

In addition to the human losses, the tsunami devastated the economy in Japan. Japan is home to many well-known companies such as Honda, Nissan, Toyota, and Sony. Because these businesses were crippled by the earthquake, many of their goods were unable to leave the factories. Business losses around the world totaled hundreds of billions of dollars.

Fukushima, Japan—One Year Later

Life is anything but back to normal on Japan's Honshu Island. Tens of thousands of families still have no permanent place to live. There is a 12-mile "No Go" zone around the power plant, and it may be expanded. Foods such as rice, beef, and fish have shown traces of radiation contamination.

And Japanese officials are worried that another earthquake or tsunami could devastate the still-vulnerable Fukushima plant.

In the meantime, scientists are taking advantage of what happened. They found radiation from the Fukushima plant in Bluefin tuna caught as far away as California. The radiation was not a threat to human health. But the scientists are using the radiation levels to track the animals, air, and water of the Pacific Ocean. It is hoped that they will learn more about migratory patterns of fish, seabirds, and ocean mammals.

DATAFILE

Timeline

July 2010

Approximately one-fifth of Pakistan's land under water from unprecedented flooding.

September 2011

Wildfires destroy close to eight hundred homes near Austin, Texas, after the hottest, driest summer in the state's recorded history.

Where is Pakistan?

HERE

Did You Know?

The country of Bangladesh is very flat and very wet. Three large rivers flow from the Himalayas and end in the bay on the southern coast. It is very likely that 30 percent of the country will be under salty sea water in the coming decades.

Key Terms

carbon dioxide—the primary greenhouse gas emitted through human activities, such as the use of fossil fuels

greenhouse gas—chemical compounds that trap heat in the lower atmosphere

methane—a colorless, odorless, flammable gas that can remain in the atmosphere for approximately 9 to 15 years; human-influenced sources include landfills, natural gas and petroleum systems, agricultural activities, coal mining, and more

CHAPTER 9 | Global Warming

Global warming refers to an increase in the earth's average temperature. Scientists believe this increase is caused by the buildup of greenhouse gases. Greenhouse gases include carbon dioxide (CO_2), which is released when burning fossil fuels like coal and oil. Carbon dioxide makes up 77 percent of our greenhouse gas emissions.

Methane is another harmful greenhouse gas. It is also released when burning fossil fuels. Methane is also produced naturally by grazing livestock and decaying organic material. It makes up 14 percent of our greenhouse gas emissions.

Global warming contributes to a number of climate-related disasters. For example, melting ice (especially glaciers) has raised sea levels. The result is more flooding, especially in lower-lying countries like Bangladesh and the Netherlands.

In 2011, the United States experienced a record 14 weather and climate emergencies. Together, these caused more than $55 billion in damage. The truth is we cannot afford global warming.

Global Warming is Different from Climate Change

Global warming refers to an increase in the earth's average temperature. Climate change involves long-term changes in several climate conditions. These include temperature, rainfall, wind, and humidity. Climate change can refer to either warming or cooling temperatures.

What Causes Global Warming?

Power plants all over the world produce most of our greenhouse gases. The generation of electricity is responsible for 40 percent of carbon dioxide emissions. Today, there are more than one billion cars and trucks on the world's roadways. They are responsible for 21 percent of our worldwide greenhouse gas emissions.

Another cause of global warming is cutting down large numbers of trees. This is called deforestation. The primary cause of the loss of the world's forests is agriculture. Trees are cut down in order to clear land to plant crops. These crops are either part of small family farms or large, commercial businesses.

The Effect on Humans

Scientists believe global warming contributes to a number of human health problems. One is heat stroke caused by heat waves. These are periods of days, or even weeks, where temperatures stay at very high levels. They are especially deadly for younger and older people. In 2003, an intense heat wave in Europe killed more than 35,000 people.

Global warming also causes an increase in wildfires by causing forests to become dryer. Wildfires contribute to air pollution. This can result in more cases of asthma and other respiratory illnesses.

Rising global temperatures devastate poor farmers. Flooding, heat waves, and drought can change a successful harvest into a disastrous one. And poor farmers depend on what they grow to feed their families. They do not have the resources needed to adapt to the effects of global warming.

Rising sea levels can lead to flooding, causing death and destruction. Millions lose their homes. Survivors of natural disasters often end up living in shelters or on the streets. They lack food, clean water, and sanitation facilities. This can lead to disease and death.

The World Health Organization estimates that diseases like malaria and malnutrition related to climate change cause 150,000 deaths each year.

The Effect on Plants and Animals

Like humans, plants and animals have gradually adapted to our changing earth. But global warming causes severe weather changes. Rainstorms can turn into devastating floods. A hot day becomes a deadly heat wave. These weather extremes make it harder for plants and animals to survive.

Global warming can change the breeding patterns of mosquitoes. In the United States, global warming could increase the number of mosquito-related diseases like West Nile Virus.

In Alaska, hot summers have led to an increase in the number of bark beetles, which are eating up millions of trees. Near the North Pole, polar bears normally live on sea ice. As this ice melts, polar bears are in danger of becoming extinct.

The loss of sea ice is the chief threat to the polar bear since it spends far more time at sea than on land. Two thirds of all polar bears may be gone by 2050.

Warmer water temperatures around the world are killing off coral reefs. Fish thrive by feeding among coral reefs. And fishermen depend on the fish for their livelihoods. When coral reefs die off, they rarely come back.

A Future in Peril

Climatologists are scientists who study long-term climate trends. They believe that if worldwide temperatures keep rising, it will be too late to stop global warming.

To reduce the effects of global warming, countries are using more green energy. These technologies include wind and solar energy. But so far, global warming is not slowing down. Carbon dioxide emissions reached an all-time high in 2011.

Currently, China is the largest producer of carbon dioxide. The United States is second. India ranks third. As our populations increase, we are using more of the earth's resources. If we want to slow global warming, each of us must reduce our usage of energy from fossil fuels.

What Can Humans Do to Help?

There are simple things we can do to help slow global warming. Turn off the lights when you leave a room. If you work on a computer, turn it off when you finish. Lower the settings on your thermostat. Walk instead of riding in a car. Even taking shorter showers helps conserve energy.

Using less energy will result in a healthier planet.

DATAFILE

Timeline

1960s

The Soviet Union diverts rivers that feed the Aral Sea to irrigate cotton and other agricultural products.

2005

The World Bank and the government of Kazakhstan built a dam to raise the water level in the North Aral to allow native fish to repopulate the sea.

Where is the Aral Sea?

HERE

Key Terms

irrigation—supplying water to land to assist in the production of crops

sediment—mineral or organic matter deposited by water, air, or ice

salinity—the relative proportion of salt in a solution

CHAPTER 10 | The Aral Sea

The Aral Sea is actually a lake. It is one of fewer than 20 ancient lakes in the world. Ancient lakes are those that have flowed constantly for more than a million years. Scientists believe that the Aral Sea is more than 5 million years old. Originally more than 26,000 square miles in size, the Aral Sea was the fourth largest lake on earth.

The Aral Sea lies between Kazakhstan and Uzbekistan. These countries used to be part of the Soviet Union.

Tens of thousands of people depended on the ancient lake for their existence. Many were fishermen. In the port town of Aralsk, people worked canning fish and building ships. Others helped transport fish to cities like Moscow. At its peak, the Aral Sea produced more than 40,000 tons of fish each year.

Today, the Aral Sea is smaller. Much smaller. The Aral has shrunk by more than 90 percent in the last 50 years. Sea levels have dropped by more than 50 feet. By 2015, some scientists believe the Aral Sea could disappear completely.

The decline of the Aral Sea has been dramatic. Before and after satellite photographs show it looking like a slowly deflating balloon. Rusted skeletons of fishing boats dot a dusty sea bed. One of the earth's great natural wonders has become one of the worst man-made environmental disasters in history.

The Aral Sea area of Central Asia has two important rivers. They are the 1,380-mile-long Syr Darya and the 1,500-mile-long Amu Darya. Both are primarily fed by melting glacier ice. Throughout history, both rivers supplied the Aral Sea with fresh water.

The destruction of the Aral Sea began in the 1960s. Planners in the Soviet Union decided to build a network of irrigation canals to grow more cotton. This would divert water from the Syr Darya and Amu Darya rivers. The Soviet plan turned out to be a historic mistake that affected millions of lives.

Cotton is a valuable crop. Socks, towels, and T-shirts are made from cotton. Even dollar bills contain cotton. But cotton crops require lots of water and fertilizer. As more water was diverted from the Syr and Amu rivers, the Aral Sea received less fresh water every year. This lack of water created high saline (salt) levels in the Aral. Eventually, the Aral Sea was saltier than an ocean.

Environmental damage in the Aral region has been severe. For 50 years, farmers have applied toxic pesticides and fertilizers to their cotton crops. These poisons leaked into surrounding watersheds (where water from different sources drains into). Marshes and wetlands started dying. Animals migrated away.

The fishing industry was especially hard hit. The Aral Sea was now too salty to sustain fish. Villagers had depended on fish as a source of protein. Without fish in their diets, families suffered from malnutrition. The port town of Aralsk was no longer on the sea. The Aral had receded so severely, the water was now over 15 miles away.

The destruction of the Aral Sea's marshes and wetlands drastically changed the area's climate. The Aral Sea and its marshes had historically helped moderate temperatures. As the Aral Sea shrank, Central Asia suffered the effects of global warming. Summers were hotter. Winters were colder.

Dried-up areas of the Aral Sea are probably lost forever. Thousands of square miles of the Aral now look like deserts. Wind storms blow toxic sediments from these deserts. Rates of respiratory disease and throat cancer in the region have increased.

Pesticide and fertilizer contamination is still a problem in watersheds around the Aral Sea. Poisons have contaminated food and drinking water. Areas around the Aral Sea now have some of the highest death rates in the former Soviet Union. But the people are too poor to move elsewhere.

Despite the destruction of the environment by humans, Mother Nature has a way of repairing herself. Today the Aral Sea is just four smaller lakes, but there are signs of recovery. The government of

Shipwreck in the desert. This abandoned ship used to be part of a thriving fishing economy in the fourth largest lake in the world.

Kazakhstan built dams that have restored water levels in what is now called the North Aral.

Higher water levels have reduced salt contamination in the North Aral Sea. Native plants are growing again, and the marshes are responding. Migrating birds like pelicans and flamingos have returned. Fishermen are out on their boats catching fish like carp and perch.

Scientists say a strong recovery for the South Aral is doubtful. It would take money and political cooperation to build dams and support the local economy. But the Aral Sea region is one of the poorest in Central Asia. At least 25 percent of its population lives below the poverty line. Scientists hope Mother Nature will help the Aral Sea and its people to recover and thrive.

Glossary

acid rain—rain that is harmful because it is mixed with polluted air

asthma—a condition that sometimes makes it hard to breathe

atomic bomb—a weapon that causes a powerful, hot explosion

carbon dioxide—the primary greenhouse gas emitted through human activities, such as the use of fossil fuels

clinic—a place where doctors examine and treat patients

contaminated—polluted or infected

extinct—no longer alive

fallout—the radioactive particles that fall after a nuclear explosion

filter—a device that makes the air or water clean

generate—to make

greenhouse gas—chemical compounds that trap heat in the lower atmosphere

industry—a business that uses machines and often produces a lot of pollution

irrigation—supplying water to land to assist in the production of crops

methane—a colorless, odorless, flammable gas that can remain in the atmosphere for approximately 9 to 15 years; human-influenced sources include landfills, natural gas and petroleum systems, agricultural activities, coal mining, and more

migratory—periodically migrating, meaning to pass from one climate or region to another

nuclear reactor—a device that produces nuclear energy

ozone layer—a part of the atmosphere that takes out some of the sun's harmful rays

pesticides—poisons used to kill animals, insects, or plants

pipeline—a long line of tubes connected together

pollution—something that harms the air, water, or soil

radiation—a form of energy that can cause cancer and other health problems

radioactive—giving off energy as a result of the break-down of atoms

reactor—a device that produces nuclear energy

reef—rock or coral that is near the water's surface

salinity—the relative proportion of salt in a solution

sediment—mineral or organic matter deposited by water, air, or ice

smog—a mixture of smoke, chemicals, and fog

subatomic—particles contained in an atom, as electrons, protons, or neutrons

tanker—a huge ship used to carry oil

toxic—very harmful

tsunami—an unusually large sea wave produced by an earthquake (In Japanese, tsu means harbor, and nami means wave.)

Union Carbide—a large company that owned the Bhopal pesticide factory

Index

acid rain, 7

Amu Darya River, 85

Aral Sea, 82, 83, 84–89

atomic bomb, 32–35

Austin, Texas, 72

Bangladesh, 73

Bhopal, 58–61

cancer, 7, 13, 23, 53, 87

carbon dioxide, 74, 80–81

Chernobyl, 52–55

Clean Air Act, 15

climate change, 75, 87

dam building, 88–89

deforestation, 76

earthquake, 65, 68, 69

flooding, 74

Fukushima Daiichi nuclear power plant, 62, 66–71

Gibbs, Lois, 25

global warming, 74–81

green energy, 80

greenhouse gases, 74, 76

Hanford, 32–37

heat waves, 77

Japan, 62, 63, 65–71

Kazakhstan, 82, 84

London, 12–15

Love Canal, 22–27

Niagara Falls, 22, 23

nuclear waste, 32, 36

oil, 42–45

Pakistan, 72

pesticides, 22, 58, 60, 86, 88

pollution, 6, 7, 12, 15, 18, 19, 71, 86, 88

Prince William Sound, 43, 45

radiation, 34–36, 53, 64, 67–68, 71

sea level, 78

smog, 13–15

Syr Darya River, 85

tsunami, 65, 68, 70

Union Carbide, 60, 61

Uzbekistan, 82, 84

Valdez, 42–45

West Nile Virus, 79

wildfires, 72, 77

World Health Organization, 78